6 Things
We Should Know About God

6 Decisions
That Will Change Your Life

Participant Workbook
DVD
Leader Guide

6 Things
We Should Know About God

Participant Workbook
DVD
Leader Guide

6 Ways
We Encounter God

Participant Workbook
DVD
Leader Guide

6 Things

We Should Know About God

Participant Workbook

Tom Berlin

with Karen Berlin

Abingdon Press
Nashville

Six Things We Should Know About God
Participant Workbook

Tom Berlin with Karen Berlin

Copyright © 2014 by Abingdon Press
All rights reserved.

This book is printed on acid-free, elemental chlorine-free paper.

ISBN 978-1-426-79456-8

Scripture quotations marked NIV are taken from the Holy Bible, New International Version®, NIV®. Copyright © 1973, 1978, 1984, 2011 by Biblica, Inc.™ Used by permission of Zondervan. All rights reserved worldwide. www.zondervan.com. The "NIV" and "New International Version" are trademarks registered in the United States Patent and Trademark Office by Biblica, Inc.™

Scripture quotations marked TNIV are taken from the Holy Bible, Today's New International Version®. Copyright © 2001, 2005. Biblica, Inc.™ All rights reserved worldwide. Used by permission of Biblica, Inc.

Scripture quotations marked NKJV are taken from the New King James Version®. Copyright © 1982 by Thomas Nelson, Inc. Used by permission. All rights reserved.

Scripture quotations marked NRSV are from the New Revised Standard Version of the Bible, copyrighted © 1989 by the Division of Christian Education of the National Council of the Churches of Christ in the United States of America, and are used by permission.

Scripture quotations marked HCSB are taken from the Holman Christian Standard Bible®, Copyright © 1999, 2000, 2002, 2003 by Holman Bible Publishers. Used by permission. Holman Christian Standard Bible®, Holman CSB®, and HCSB® are federally registered trademarks of Holman Bible Publishers.

14 15 16 17 18 19 20 21 22 23—10 9 8 7 6 5 4 3 2 1
MANUFACTURED IN THE UNITED STATES OF AMERICA

With God's help, I will draw closer to Christ through this six-week study as I commit to read the Bible and prayerfully reflect on its meaning for my life.

_____

My Name

_____

Start Date

Contents

Welcome!

We're glad you are participating in *Six Things We Should Know About God*. When you commit yourself to this six-week journey, we believe you will grow deeper in your relationship with Christ. You will gain the most from this study if you make the following practices a part of your journey:

1. **Attend a small group.** Your church offers small group opportunities where spiritual transformation can be encouraged and enhanced through community. Those gathered will have the opportunity to share and discuss their insights, questions, and life experiences and, most importantly, to apply lessons learned about their personal and corporate study. The study includes, in addition to this Participant Workbook, a DVD and Leader Guide to enhance learning and group involvement. We encourage all to join a small group for this study.

2. **Use the Participant Workbook five days a week.** This book is intended to draw you into a daily conversation with God by guiding you in reading key Scripture passages, responding to reflective questions, and journaling your thoughts about how this encounter applies to your life.

3. **Attend worship.** Our conversation with God is incomplete if we don't participate in individual and corporate worship. Go to church every week, but during the study make a special point of attending.

How to Use This Book

When you use this book each day, begin your time with prayer. Read the Bible passages assigned for the day. Answer the questions provided, journal on your own, or do a combination of these two options.

Write out a Scripture verse that speaks to you from the assigned reading. It may be a verse of encouragement, instruction, confession, or insight.

Observe what the verse says, and write a few sentences about its relevance to your life.

Relate the text to your life by applying it to a specific issue you are considering, a problem you are facing, or an encouragement God wants you to hear. Write a short paragraph in which you share what you are hearing from God's Word.

Decide to share with God the desire of your heart. As a result of reading this text, what do you want to do and who do you want to become? Share your thoughts by writing a short prayer to conclude your conversation with God.

God Loves You

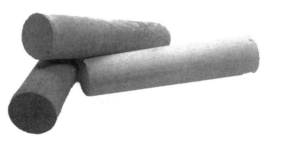

Day 1

Today's Scripture
Psalm 139:1-18; 1 John 3:1-3

Key Verse

*I praise you because I am fearfully and wonderfully made;
your works are wonderful, I know that full well.*

Psalm 139:14 NIV

1. In Psalm 139:7-12, what is the psalmist teaching about God's presence with us?

_____

_____

_____

_____

_____

2. What does it mean to see yourself as a child of God?

_____

_____

_____

_____

_____

Going Deeper

This psalm features King David singing about the wonders of God. David celebrates because while God knows the whole universe, God also knows and loves him intimately. This text, which we read, was sung in biblical times as a popular song of celebration and an act of praise. The message still resounds today: God knows all of us from our first breath to our eternal life.

There are countless things in Creation, but God specifically cares not only about our names but our lives, our struggles, and our joys as well. God is working for our good but gives us the choice to follow or to go our own way.

David chose to respond to God's offer of a loving relationship with praise, and his life was blessed for his obedience. David's psalm pushes us to consider how we will choose to live.

Trivia Tidbit

According to BBC Science, when first "knit together" in the mother's womb, a baby has around 300 bone parts. Some bones fuse together over time, and by adulthood we end up with 206 bones.

Going Deeper Questions

3. God is aware of all our ways and knows our words before we speak them. How does that thought make you feel about God? How can God know our thoughts and futures and yet still give us free will?

_____

_____

_____

_____

_____

4. "What we will be has not yet been made known" (1 John 3:2). As Christians, we do not know everything about heaven, but we do know that we will have a "spiritual body" and live in a perfect relationship with God and others. What does that mean? What will it be like then, and how should we be striving for it now?

_____

_____

_____

_____

_____

Day 2

Today's Scripture
Romans 8

Key Verse

For you did not receive the spirit of bondage again to fear, but you received the Spirit of adoption by whom we cry out, "Abba, Father."

Romans 8:15 NKJV

1. Paul begins this passage with these words of encouragement: "There is therefore now no condemnation to those who are in Christ Jesus." What does this phrase mean to you?

_____

_____

_____

_____

2. Read verse 15 aloud three times. How does this statement make you feel?

_____

_____

_____

_____

Going Deeper

Adoption in the ancient world was a big deal, just as it is today. It was an important legal proceeding with witnesses. Those who adopted someone entrusted this child with their good name and reputation, as well a portion of their inheritance. Usually, this process involved the symbolic selling of the adopted person to the new parent. Thus, the adopted person was bought with a price and officially made a part of the family.

Paul tells us that God has taken this a step further, not only adopting us but also making us co-heirs to the kingdom. Not only that, we are invited to call God *Abba*, which is an Aramaic term meaning not just Father, but "Dad" or "Daddy."

We are invited to relate to God as we would to a loving parent. Children often do not understand or value the sacrifices parents make for them. This may be why in his letters Paul calls Christians to greater maturity. As we mature, we understand all that God has done to offer a relationship to us, just as adult children understand all their parents did for them over the years.

> ### Trivia Tidbit
> *The Holy Spirit is referred to about twenty times in Romans 8 alone. That's sixteen more times than in the first seven chapters of Romans combined!*

Going Deeper Questions

3. The price of our adoption was the death of Jesus Christ, God in human form, and yet we are allowed to call God our *"Abba,* Father." How will you celebrate and thank God for the love Christ showed us on the cross?

_____

_____

_____

_____

_____

_____

_____

4. What does it mean to "walk according to the Spirit" in our everyday lives? What does it teach us about people?

_____

_____

_____

_____

_____

_____

_____

Day 3

Today's Scripture

Matthew 5:1-12; 6:25-34

Key Verse

But seek first his kingdom and his righteousness, and all these things will be given to you as well.

Matthew 6:33 NIV

1. In today's Scripture, consider the word *blessed*. What distinguishes being "blessed" from being "happy"?

_____

_____

_____

_____

2. Worry is a troublesome cancer that removes God's peace in the lives of many of us. God's antidote to worry is for us to trust. State in your own words the trust Christ offers in Matthew 6:33.

_____

_____

_____

_____

Going Deeper

Don't worry. Be happy. It seems a bit too easy, doesn't it? With so much going on in our lives, it seems almost impossible just to let go and not worry about all the things that could go wrong.

At the beginning of the Sermon on the Mount, Jesus promises help and blessings for those who trust in the Lord, regardless of how their lives are going. Those who hunger will be filled. Those who are persecuted will be rewarded. Those who forgive will be forgiven. When we try to hold onto our plans and fret about all the things that could happen, we lose the blessing of depending on God as our provider.

Because we know we can't control the outcomes and impact of our decisions, we worry. Jesus asks us to let go of the worry so that he can take care of things. We will find ourselves in tough situations sometimes, but when we rely on God and trust God enough to be obedient, many things will work out through God's blessings.

Trivia Tidbit

Though rendered as "blessed" in most translations of the Beatitudes, the Greek word makarios *can also mean "happy," "fortunate," or "prosperous."*

Going Deeper Questions

3. Which area of the Beatitudes do you feel best able to live out? Which one feels difficult? What might assist you in gaining the blessings that Jesus speaks of here?

_____

_____

4. Is being "blessed" an action that can be experienced multiple times or a continual state of being? How can a blessing be lost or taken away?

_____

_____

5. What is the difference between planning for the future and worrying?

_____

_____

6. What do you worry about more: things you can control or things you cannot? What methods have you found that enable you to leave your anxiety in God's hands?

_____

_____

_____

Day 4

Today's Scripture
Luke 15

Key Verse

So he got up and went to his father. But while he was still a long way off, his father saw him and was filled with compassion for him; he ran to his son, threw his arms around him and kissed him.

Luke 15:20 NIV

1. In the Parable of the Lost Son, what do you learn about the heart of the father as you contrast his responses to the elder and younger sons?

_____

_____

_____

_____

2. Why do you think the father's view of the lost son is so different from the son's view of himself in this story?

_____

_____

_____

_____

Going Deeper

The Parable of the Lost Son, also called the Parable of the Prodigal Son, is well known, but we don't usually think of what the words mean. By definition, *prodigal* means extravagant or lavish, which is a good description of the son in this story.

However, the word can also refer to the father in this situation, a man who was extravagant in his love and forgiveness despite the wrongs he had suffered. The son, in asking for his portion of the inheritance, had communicated that his inheritance was more important to him than his father was. Essentially, the son was saying that his father's life was getting in the way of the inheritance. In any culture this would be hurtful and insulting. Amazingly, the father gave the son his portion.

> **Trivia Tidbit**
>
> *The silver coin in the Parable of the Lost Coin was a Greek* drachma, *which was equal to one day's wage and was nearly equivalent to the* Roman denarius.

More amazing still, when the son squandered the money and came crawling back, the father was there to welcome him home. The father restored his son to the family he had left. The father even threw a party for the boy and rejoiced that his son had come home, displaying an extravagant love that seemed to know no bounds.

We too can be prodigal sons and daughters, wandering far away. But we have a prodigal father who is full of compassion and abounding in love. The father in this parable showed remarkable grace. He gave his son forgiveness that was not earned, with no strings attached.

Going Deeper Questions

3. What is the most important person or thing in your life? What would you do if you lost that person or thing? What would you do to get it back?

_____

_____

_____

4. In the three parables in Luke 15, notice how in each case the finder (of the sheep, the coin, and the son) called the people together and rejoiced extravagantly. Describe some times you celebrated because people who had been lost were found or came to their senses.

_____

_____

_____

5. We often forget that in the Parable of the Lost Son, there were two sinful sons: the one who went away from the father and the one who stayed with the father but harbored inward sins such as pride and bitterness. Which son do you relate to, and how can all of us learn from our mistakes to be better children of God?

_____

_____

_____

Day 5

Key Verse

But speaking the truth in love, we must grow up in every way into him who is the head, into Christ.

Ephesians 4:15 NRSV

1. At the beginning of today's Scripture, what is Paul urging the readers of his letter to do?

_____

_____

_____

_____

_____

2. What does it mean in verses 22-24 to "put away" and to "clothe your-selves"? What is one way you have experienced this contrast in your faith journey so far?

_____

_____

_____

_____

_____

Going Deeper

Paul often describes the church as "the body of Christ," an amalgamation of parts with different strengths and purposes that come together to form one spiritual unit. He means that God has made each one of us in such a way that we have something different to offer one another and the ministry of the church.

When we contribute our time and talents to the church, we truly give it a gift. God is blessing the church through each of us. When we fail to participate, the body as a whole suffers, because each of us has an important role, and each of our gifts contributes to the whole.

If God has taken the effort to fashion each of us in such a way that we have something to offer, then each of us really is one of God's favorite children. You are as irreplaceable in your church as a child is in a family.

Trivia Tidbit

Ephesus appears in six books of the New Testament (Acts, 1 Corinthians, Ephesians, 1 and 2 Timothy, and Revelation) and is traditionally believed to be the final resting place of the apostle John.

Going Deeper Questions

3. According to Paul, what is necessary for the church to be unified as a body?

_____

_____

_____

_____

4. Think of someone who is a spiritual mentor to you. What gifts of the Spirit do you see in that person, and how are those gifts expressed?

_____

_____

_____

_____

5. What gifts do you feel that God has blessed you with, and how can you better use these gifts to serve?

_____

_____

_____

_____

Week Two

God
Understands You

Day 1

Today's Scripture
Psalm 8; Genesis 1:27-31

Key Verse
O LORD, our Sovereign, how majestic is your name in all the earth! You have set your glory above the heavens.

Psalm 8:1 NRSV

1. How is God described in Psalm 8?

_____

_____

_____

_____

_____

2. In Genesis 1:27-31, what is God's perspective on humans and their place in creation? What is your response to the place humans are given in that account?

_____

_____

_____

_____

_____

Going Deeper

One difficulty in trying to understand God is the "both/and" nature of the Creator.

God is a being who understands both the photosynthetic processes that keep plants alive and the astrophysics that keep galaxies moving. God can handle the fine craftsmanship of butterfly wings and the mass of planets, suns, and moons. The psalmist is in awe of this when he writes, "What are human beings that you are mindful of them, mortals that you care for them?" (8:4).

This is the both/and part of God's character. The one who created the universe also knows the number of hairs on your head. Thinking of a God who created everything but who still knows every single one of us can only lead to a worshipful, awe-stricken reverence.

Trivia Tidbit

Eden was located in the Fertile Crescent, the location usually credited with domesticating animals and the invention of writing and the wheel.

31

Going Deeper Questions

3. What does it mean that God's name is "majestic"? If you were writing a psalm, what words would you use to praise God?

_____

_____

_____

_____

4. God's glory is shown in all of creation. Where do you personally see God's nature at work in creation, in humanity, and in the processes of the universe? How often do you think about those things and praise God for them?

_____

_____

_____

_____

5. As those who have been given "dominion over the works of [God's] hands," what is our responsibility in caring for one another and for the rest of God's creation?

_____

_____

_____

Day 2

Today's Scripture
John 15:1-17

Key Verse

I am the vine; you are the branches. If you remain in me and I in you, you will bear much fruit; apart from me you can do nothing.

John 15:5 NIV

1. In response to the key verse, finish this statement: "If Jesus is the vine, and I am the branch, then that means . . ."

_____

_____

_____

_____

2. A right relationship with God is not about what we do for God, but much more about what God does within and through us. Explain the difference between these two perspectives. Which is more descriptive of your relationship with God?

_____

_____

_____

_____

Going Deeper

In Jesus' time, a vineyard was a symbol of health and nourishment. Water was often scarce or contaminated, so grapes were grown in vineyards to produce wine for drinking. Jesus' audience would have been well acquainted with the idea of gardening vines to create good grapes for winemaking, including the pruning of dead limbs and the attaching of more fruitful ones in their place.

In the Old Testament, Israel is sometimes represented as a vine, a chosen people through whom God would nourish the rest of the world. By claiming to be the true vine, Jesus was saying that he was the culmination of that prophecy—the one who would save the world and bring it health and happiness. At the Last Supper, he made it even clearer by saying that the wine from this true vine was his blood, the blood of the new and everlasting covenant.

Jesus understood that we need a source of nourishment and strength beyond ourselves if we are going to experience health and be fruitful over time.

Trivia Tidbit

According to the online Encyclopedia Romana, in ancient times wine was often mixed with two to four measures of water, and it was considered uncouth to drink undiluted wine (which was called merum*).*

Going Deeper Questions

3. A branch must be nourished by the vine to make fruit. What can we do to be nourished by Christ?

_____

_____

_____

4. What does it mean to "bear fruit" for Christ? What kind of fruit are you bearing, and where do you see an opportunity to bear more?

_____

_____

_____

5. Both good and bad branches in this story get cut and trimmed in the pruning process. The fruitful branches are pruned to become even more fruitful; the fruitless branches are stagnant and are cut off completely. How can we live a life in Christ that will lead to fruitfulness rather than stagnation?

_____

_____

_____

_____

35

Day 3

Today's Scripture
Isaiah 53

Key Verse

But he was pierced for our transgressions, he was crushed for our iniquities; the punishment that brought us peace was on him, and by his wounds we are healed.

Isaiah 53:5 TNIV

1. In your own words, write what we learn about Christ in Isaiah 53:11-12.

_____

_____

_____

_____

_____

2. Based on what you know about the Christian faith and what you have read in this passage, how would you explain the meaning of Christ's death and resurrection to someone else?

_____

_____

_____

_____

_____

Going Deeper

In the Old Testament, prophets were called by God to challenge people in authority and to question accepted practices of the larger population. Prophets would point out missteps by the nation of Israel, call the people back to obedience, and pray for the salvation of the land.

Being a prophet was a difficult job. No one wanted to have faults pointed out or to be criticized for actions in front of others. Kings and crowds alike often became violent with the prophets of God. Some prophets even lost their lives.

> **Trivia Tidbit**
>
> *Researcher Joel Kalvesmaki calculates that Isaiah is quoted or referred to in 14 of the 27 New Testament books, 66 times in total, 13 of those by Jesus himself.*

There was another side to the work of the prophet. Some got to hear God's intention for the future. The old Testament prophet Isaiah was a good example. He was widely quoted in the New Testament. This passage in particular built a bridge between the prophecies about the destruction of Jerusalem and the salvation that a Messiah would bring.

The message of a coming Messiah was a message of hope, a message that God understood the problem of sin and proposed a new way of life.

Going Deeper Questions

3. It is clear from reading the Gospels that Jesus knew his life would end on a cross and would be a sacrifice for the sins of humanity. What kind of thoughts do you imagine went through Jesus' mind as he considered both a human fear of death and a divine love for humanity?

_____

_____

_____

_____

_____

4. How does the knowledge of Isaiah's prophecy, fulfilled in the suffering and death of Jesus, affect your life?

_____

_____

_____

_____

_____

Day 4

Key Verse

God is spirit, and those who worship him must worship in spirit and truth.

John 4:24 NRSV

1. What do you think Jesus meant in verse 10 by the term "living water"?

_____

_____

_____

_____

_____

2. How did the Samaritan woman react to her encounter with Jesus? Why do you think she responded in that way?

_____

_____

_____

_____

_____

Going Deeper

In Jesus' culture, there were many reasons why he wouldn't be expected to speak with a Samaritan woman. There was a standing feud between the Jews and the Samaritans. Samaritans were considered unclean because they were a result of intermarrying when the Assyrians conquered Israel in 722 B.C. Women were seen to have a lesser status than men in that society, so it would be out of the ordinary for a man to talk with a woman he did not know, much less to accept food or drink from her.

However, Jesus had a way of breaking down barriers among people. He knew things about this woman that she did not like to admit. While he recognized the Samaritan woman's deepest sins, he did not make her feel condemned. He spoke to her in a way that encouraged her to live a new life. As a result, she became a great witness to his love and brought other members of her community to meet Jesus.

> **Trivia Tidbit**
>
> *According to* The Interpreter's Dictionary of the Bible, *the term "living water" was commonly used to refer to moving water in a stream as opposed to standing water in a well or pond.*

Going Deeper Questions

3. In his encounter with the Samaritan woman, Jesus asked for a simple thing—a drink of water—and yet, for a number of reasons, she balked at his request. Describe a time when you ignored a calling of God or made excuses for not doing what God may have wanted you to do.

_____

_____

_____

_____

_____

_____

4. What lessons can we take from Jesus' love for the lost and the Samaritan woman's zeal for bringing others to the Lord? How can we follow their examples?

_____

_____

_____

_____

_____

_____

Day 5

Key Verse

I am confident of this, that the one who began a good work among you will bring it to completion by the day of Jesus Christ.

Philippians 1:6 NRSV

1. What are the components of Paul's prayer in verses 9-11 of today's Scripture?

_____

_____

_____

_____

2. How might Paul's words and example in verses 12-14 encourage you, or someone you know, in the midst of difficult circumstances?

_____

_____

_____

_____

_____

Going Deeper

The book of Philippians finds Paul writing a letter from prison . . . again.

The church in Philippi was a constant source of encouragement to Paul. They sent him support while he was in prison and were partners in his ministry when he planted churches. In his letter, Paul expressed deep gratitude for their friendship through the years of his ministry. Paul, who had been their pastor, encouraging the growth of their faith in Christ, wanted them to know that he was confident God would carry their work to its completion.

Paul was aware that there were many who were dividing the church with false messages. However, he was certain that the love of Christ would guide the Philippian Christians to care for one another, hold to a genuine faith, and continue to mature as Christ followers.

Paul's gratitude for their "sharing in the gospel" must have been a source of hope and encouragement while he was locked in prison.

Trivia Tidbit

In 1:13 Paul indicates that he is writing Philippians from the custody of the praetorium. Easton's Illustrated Bible Dictionary *explains that this could mean a military base or even the governor's palace.*

43

Going Deeper Questions

3. Paul's relationship with the Philippian church was warm, friendly, and intimate. He conferred with them and prayed with them even from afar. In what ways can our church life today emulate that of Paul and the Philippians?

_____

_____

_____

_____

_____

_____

4. In prison Paul learned to give thanks in all circumstances. He believed that he was able to glorify God in prison as easily as he could as a free man. Why is it sometimes so hard for us to give thanks to God, even in much easier situations? How can we give glory to God in our daily lives?

_____

_____

_____

_____

_____

_____

Week Three

God Forgives You

Day 1

Today's Scripture

Luke 5:1-11

Key Verse

When Simon Peter saw this, he fell at Jesus' knees and said, "Go away from me, Lord; I am a sinful man!"

Luke 5:8 NIV

1. Contrast Simon's response in verse 5 of today's Scripture to his response in verse 8. What is different in the way he addressed Jesus?

_____

_____

_____

_____

2. Simon experienced his own sinfulness and unworthiness when he recognized Jesus as Lord. Why is recognizing our sinfulness an important aspect of understanding and accepting Christ?

_____

_____

_____

_____

_____

Going Deeper

Rabbis were the philosophers and teachers of Jewish society. Often they would take on a small group of students to instruct in their understanding of God and Scripture.

In today's Scripture, Jesus was selecting some of his disciples in a very unusual way. Peter and his friends had been fishing all night. They had had no success and were tired and hungry from their efforts when this rabbi told them to lower their nets into the water again. Rabbis were respected for many things, but fishing advice was rarely on the list. In deference to Jesus, however, they did as he said, and a miracle occurred. Suddenly they had more fish than they could handle.

Trivia Tidbit

According to historian Mendel Nun, the net in this passage was probably a linen trammel net, which was used at night (when the fish couldn't see it) and had to be dried on the beach between uses.

Peter recognized that Jesus was no ordinary rabbi; he was a powerful man of God who could perform miracles. Peter experienced awe and even fear as he knelt before Jesus.

When Jesus asked the fishermen to join him, they realized this was the offer of a lifetime. They did not feel worthy, but they understood the opportunity before them. Leaving everything, they went off to begin a new life with Jesus.

Going Deeper Questions

3. Why did Simon tell Jesus to go away when he recognized Jesus' power and authority? Why didn't he instead ask Jesus to stay with them?

_____

_____

_____

_____

_____

_____

_____

4. Describe a time in your life when you had to make some real changes in order to follow Jesus.

_____

_____

_____

_____

_____

_____

_____

Day 2

Key Verse

Thanks be to God through Jesus Christ our Lord! So then, with my mind I am a slave to the law of God, but with my flesh I am a slave to the law of sin.

Romans 7:25 NRSV

1. In verse 4 of today's Scripture, what point is Paul trying to make regarding the law, Christ's death, and us?

_____

_____

_____

_____

2. Express in your own words the dilemma Paul describes in verses 14-20. In whom did Paul find the answer to this battle that raged within him?

_____

_____

_____

_____

_____

Going Deeper

The Law of Moses provided the foundation of Hebrew culture in Jesus' time. The first five books of the Old Testament are called the Pentateuch and contain both the Law and the record of the first covenants God made with the people of Israel. Much of this Law was given to create order in their society. To us the Law sometimes seems too detailed, but it was designed to protect God's people. For example, the dietary requirement of avoiding shellfish may seem silly now, but when you live in a desert with no way to safely transport or store raw seafood, it is understandable why the Law instructed people to avoid this type of food.

> ### Trivia Tidbit
> *Paul's word for "opportunity" in verse 8 refers to a military embankment from which an army could mount an attack on an enemy.*

Paul wrote about his experience of wrestling with the Law. As a Pharisee, he was an expert on its meaning. He knew the details. He wanted to be obedient to it. But there was something inside him that resisted being obedient. He knew the Law in his mind but did not keep it in his heart, which was the seat of his inner will. As such, the Law served only to define longings for disobedience to God.

Paul found release from this destructive cycle in the love of Jesus Christ. He believed in Jesus as the Messiah because Jesus had set Paul free of his bondage to sin.

Going Deeper Questions

3. What does it mean in verse 2 that we are "discharged from the law"? Surely, it can't mean we can do whatever we want.

_____

_____

4. What is the "new life of the Spirit" as compared with the "old written code" (verse 6)?

_____

_____

5. Sometimes people say "The Devil made me do it" as a way of avoiding responsibility. It seems unlikely that Paul would try to evade his obligation to God. So what does he mean in verse 17 when he says, "But in fact it is no longer I that do it, but sin that dwells within me"?

_____

_____

6. All Christians have places in their lives where they know what is right and want to do it but often fall short. Where do you struggle, and why do you think we have trouble doing what is right even when we know what is right?

_____

_____

Day 3

Today's Scripture
John 8:1-11

Key Verse

"Then neither do I condemn you," Jesus declared. "Go now and leave your life of sin."

John 8:11b NIV

1. In today's Scripture, why did the religious leaders bring the adulterous woman to Jesus and put her on public display, and what was Jesus' response to their questions in verse 7?

_____

_____

_____

_____

2. With whom do you most identify in this passage? Why?

_____

_____

_____

_____

Going Deeper

By Hebrew law, the incident in today's Scripture should have been an open-and-shut case. Leviticus declared that those caught in adultery by witnesses should die. But for Jesus, there was a lot more going on in this case than a desire for obedience to the Law.

Be aware that under Roman rule, the Israelites were not allowed to pursue capital punishment without permission of the Roman authorities. Given this fact, why was Jesus being asked to decide whether to end this woman's life? The answer is that the situation was not about adultery or obedience; it was about trapping Jesus. The people who brought the woman there wanted Jesus to appear either too timid to punish sin or too eager to break the laws of Roman rule.

In response, Jesus made the crowd do its own thinking. He told them to throw their stones if they were without sin. In that moment, all you could hear was the sound of rocks falling to the ground. That left Jesus, the only person without sin, to speak to the woman. Jesus forgave the woman her sin but told her, "Go your way, and from now on do not sin again."

Trivia Tidbit

Once a year, the Jewish high priest was allowed to go into God's presence in the Temple, but only after he had been cleansed of sin through sacrifices and purification.

Then and now, Jesus has a way of acting in grace and love while still calling us to obey God in a way that is infinitely more effective than the condemnation of others.

Going Deeper Questions

3. What do you think Jesus was writing in the dirt that made people stop and reconsider the situation?

_____

_____

_____

_____

_____

4. Jesus saved the woman in this story, forgiving her sins but also telling her not to sin again. How do you react to others when you see them doing things they will later regret? How does Jesus' example challenge you to act in those situations?

_____

_____

_____

_____

_____

_____

Day 4

Today's Scripture

Luke 7:36-50

Key Verse

Therefore, I tell you, her sins, which were many, have been forgiven; hence she has shown great love. But the one to whom little is forgiven, loves little.

Luke 7:47 NRSV

1. What was Jesus saying to Simon in the story about the two men who owed money?

_____

_____

_____

_____

_____

2. Reading about Jesus' response to this woman, how do you react when Christ responds to you in the same way—seeing your ultimate potential and forgiving you of your sins?

_____

_____

_____

_____

Going Deeper

Jesus and the Pharisees sometimes didn't get along very well, because they had very different agendas. The Pharisees were a sect of Judaism who tried to follow every detail of the Mosaic Law and looked down on those who did not share their zeal, or worse yet, who were found committing some sin. Jesus, by contrast, came to make God available to everyone, to forgive sins, and to offer people new life.

> **Trivia Tidbit**
>
> *People in Jesus' time often ate while lying on their sides with their feet pulled behind them. Low couches could be placed by the table for comfort.*

It's not surprising, therefore, that when the woman began to wash Jesus' feet, Jesus and a Pharisee had very different reactions. The Pharisee focused on her past. He assumed that she was a common person if she was willing to touch Jesus' feet and use her hair to dry them. This task was something that a servant would do. Using one's hands and hair to accomplish the task would have been seen as unclean.

The Pharisee may have assumed that the woman had a troubled past. Jesus saw her future. She was offering her best to him, anointing him with ointment and humbly washing his feet, something no one else was willing to do. By looking to her future, Jesus was able to announce her forgiveness and encourage her to lead a new life.

Going Deeper Questions

3. Both Simon and the woman in this passage had the chance to honor Jesus as he was welcomed into this home. Only the "sinful" woman took it. How can we follow her example today and honor Christ in our lives?

_____

_____

_____

_____

_____

4. The woman's humble actions and poignant love were a way of requesting forgiveness. It is easy to take forgiveness for granted. What does this passage teach us about seeking forgiveness from God in our lives today?

_____

_____

_____

_____

_____

_____

Day 5

Today's Scripture
Galatians 5

Key Verse

For the entire law is fulfilled in keeping this one command: "Love your neighbor as yourself."

Galatians 5:14 TNIV

1. To what is Paul referring in verse 9 when he quotes the proverb, "A little yeast works through the whole batch of dough"?

_____

_____

_____

_____

_____

2. If rule-keeping is not the means by which we can please God and live in a right relationship with God, what is?

_____

_____

_____

_____

_____

Going Deeper

Circumcision is an important matter in the Bible, but for some of us it is an odd process to understand. Why would God command that men undergo such a procedure in order to be a part of God's chosen people?

To make sense of it, we need to understand the idea of a covenant. God made a promise to Israel that they would be the chosen people, a people that God protected and blessed. In return, the Israelites promised to serve and worship only God. In that time, a sign or seal was often used to represent an oath. In this case, circumcision acted as a physical sign that a man had promised to worship only the Lord and keep the commandments of the God of Israel.

Circumcision was performed on the most intimate region of a man. It was a symbol that God had claimed all of the man, even where he was most vulnerable.

Paul said, however, that because of the new covenant in Christ, men no longer had

> **Trivia Tidbit**
>
> *The Greek word for "joy"—*chara*—comes from the same root word as the word for "grace"—*charis.

to be circumcised. Their salvation would be in Christ alone. Paul's desire was that people would still allow themselves to be claimed by God and experience a "circumcision" of the heart.

Discussing circumcision may be awkward, but it brings up a good question: How committed are we to our covenant with God?

Going Deeper Questions

3. What does Paul mean in verse 16 when he says to "walk by the Spirit"?
   How can we give ourselves over to the Spirit in our everyday lives?

   _____

   _____

   _____

   _____

   _____

   _____

   _____

4. In today's Scripture, we are told to avoid doing bad things and to strive
   for good fruit. What do you think is a healthy balance between giving
   God control and striving to do good for God?

   _____

   _____

   _____

   _____

   _____

   _____

Week Four

God Wants You to Be Free

61

Day 1

Key Verse

And the LORD God said, "The man has now become like one of us, knowing good and evil. He must not be allowed to reach out his hand and take also from the tree of life and eat, and live forever."

Genesis 3:22 NIV

1. What did Adam and Eve experience after eating the fruit? What act of grace did God extend toward them, even in the midst of sin?

_____

_____

_____

_____

2. Rather than run to God and confess what had happened, Adam and Eve ran away from God and hid. Why is confession or saying "I'm sorry" so difficult? Is your experience with sin similar to this or different? Why?

_____

_____

_____

_____

Going Deeper

It seems strange to think of a world where we wouldn't know good from evil. Why wouldn't God want us to know the difference? It seems like such knowledge is useful and necessary, but we have to consider what it was like in the Garden before the Fall.

Adam and Eve's world was as perfect a place as you could imagine. Food was in abundance. God cared for the inhabitants and communed with Adam and Eve directly, even "walking" with them. They were naked, and yet they felt no shame because they had nothing to hide. They knew God and each other intimately, so there was nothing that needed to be concealed. Sin and death weren't even present in this world. So it wasn't a matter of not knowing the difference between good and evil; it was a matter of evil not even existing yet.

> **Trivia Tidbit**
>
> *The Bible describes cherubim as having four faces (lion, ox, eagle, human), four wings, and (sometimes) a flaming sword— a far cry from the winged babies of Renaissance art.*

That is what changed with Adam and Eve's disobedience. For the first time they knew that evil existed, and for the first time they felt shame. They had something to hide from each other, and they felt a need to conceal themselves from God.

It is interesting that the Hebrew *shema*, or great commandment, is to "Love the LORD your God with all your heart and with all your soul and with all your strength" (Deuteronomy 6:5). Jesus said that the second greatest commandment was to "love your neighbor as yourself" (Matthew 22:39). These are the two things that God has been trying to recreate ever since evil was first embraced by humanity.

Going Deeper Questions

3. In today's Scripture, how did the serpent tempt Eve? In what ways is this similar to the temptations that face you?

_____

_____

_____

_____

_____

_____

4. This is the first occurrence of relational strife recorded in the Bible, both with God and between Adam and Eve. How does sin affect each of these relationships? How does it affect relationships in your life?

_____

_____

_____

_____

_____

_____

_____

Day 2

Today's Scripture
Deuteronomy 30

Key Verse

Love the LORD your God, obey Him, and remain faithful to Him. For He is your life, and He will prolong your life in the land the LORD swore to give to your fathers Abraham, Isaac, and Jacob.

Deuteronomy 30:20 HCSB

1. What do you think were the main dangers to the covenant described in today's Scripture? What other gods, besides the Lord, might they have been tempted to serve?

_____

_____

_____

2. What other "gods" tempt you and replace God as lord of your life?

_____

_____

_____

_____

Going Deeper

During their history, the Jewish people have experienced hardships, exile, and independence. Though they were God's chosen people, they often chose to go against God's plans, both politically and spiritually, bowing to kings and idols instead of to God. As a result, God often let them experience the consequences of their own plans, when their alliances with other kings and false religions separated them from God and their homeland.

> ## Trivia Tidbit
>
> *The term* diaspora, *from a Greek word meaning "a scattering," can describe the situation of the Hebrews in exile after conquest by the Assyrians, the Babylonians, or the Roman Empire.*

Today's Scripture speaks of maintaining hope even in such times. God promised the children of Israel a way back, even when they least deserved it.

And so it is with us. Certainly there are times when we have fallen away from God through our actions. But we always have the opportunity to return from our self-imposed exile. By God's grace, we can come back through the new covenant offered by Christ.

Going Deeper Questions

3. What areas in your life are stumbling blocks that get in the way of making good decisions?

_____

_____

_____

_____

_____

_____

4. We are told to love God with all our heart and all our soul. What does that mean? What is the difference between the two, and what does it look like to love that way?

_____

_____

_____

_____

_____

Day 3

Today's Scripture

John 1

Key Verse

The Word became flesh and made his dwelling among us. We have seen his glory, the glory of the one and only [Son], who came from the Father, full of grace and truth.

John 1:14 TNIV

1. In today's Scripture, contrast verses 10-11 with verses 12-13. What does the passage say about those who believed?

_____

_____

_____

_____

_____

2. How would your life be different if you did not have the understanding of Christ that you have right now?

_____

_____

_____

_____

Going Deeper

John the Gospel writer began his account of Jesus' life by poetically describing who Jesus was and what he meant to the people. John called him "the Word," from the Greek word *logos*, which meant wisdom, or a principle that gave meaning to the world.

All of this was fairly abstract until John personified this eternal Word as the Christ who had come down to earth. Imagine how excited people would have been with that announcement. This was the Messiah that prophets had talked about for generations.

The Gospel writer then connected the Son of God to a prophet of his time, John the Baptist. This would have made perfect sense to the hearers and readers of this Gospel. God often prepared the way for great events by sending prophets who could explain the events in a way that people could understand.

Finally, there was the action described in this passage. Baptism was only required for Gentiles who converted to Judaism, but John showed that everyone needed to be cleansed of their sin and baptized into the grace of God. Readers and hearers of this book would have thought about the crowds John baptized and remembered the sense of expectancy that everyone felt. John let them know that God was doing something that would change everything.

Trivia Tidbit

John is the only one of the four Gospels that doesn't include the temptation of Jesus or the sharing of bread and wine at the Last Supper, but it alone describes the wedding at Cana and Jesus raising Lazarus from the dead.

Going Deeper Questions

3. How is the beginning of John's Gospel different from the start of the other Gospels? What parts of it would have seemed shocking to John's audience back then? How does it strike you now?

_____

_____

_____

_____

_____

_____

_____

4. Several people in this story saw or heard about Jesus' baptism: John, the Pharisees, the disciples. How did each react to it? How do you react to Jesus and his unique existence as both God and man?

_____

_____

_____

_____

_____

_____

Day 4

Today's Scripture
Colossians 1

Key Verse

But now he has reconciled you by Christ's physical body through death to present you holy in his sight, without blemish and free from accusation.

Colossians 1:22 NIV

1. What does Paul describe as hallmarks of a healthy church?

_____

_____

_____

_____

2. If you were born and raised in the church, what keeps you connected? If you were not, what brought you into the life of the church, and why are you still connected?

_____

_____

_____

_____

_____

Going Deeper

"Reconciling" is the act of restoring harmony, often in the area of relationships. God is perfect and holy. That is why our sinfulness creates such a distance from God's presence. Our God is a perfect God, and therefore no sin can enter his presence . . . which is a problem, since all of us have sinned at one time or another.

Paul affirms that in the beginning Christ was with God. All things were created through him. This is why Jesus has the power to reconcile us to himself through his death, which paid for our sins and provides the offer of forgiveness and reconciliation.

> **Trivia Tidbit**
>
> *The city of Colossae was so involved in the weaving industry that it had a type of red-dyed cloth named after it.*

We can choose to ask for this forgiveness. But we must then choose to remain steadfast in our faith rather than return to our old life, in which our sin created such a distance from God. Rather than shift away from hope in Christ, Paul calls us to a life of holiness, where we mature as God's children, growing up in the likeness of our Creator.

Going Deeper Questions

3. What parts of Paul's prayer affect you the most? What parts do you pray for yourself, and what parts do you pray for others?

_____

_____

_____

_____

4. What does Paul mean in verse 24 when he writes, "I fill up in my flesh what is still lacking in regard to Christ's afflictions"? How does our perseverance in hard times bring glory to God?

_____

_____

_____

_____

5. What does it mean to be reconciled by Christ? How have you seen that process at work in your life?

_____

_____

_____

_____

Day 5

Key Verse

But Jesus looked at them and said to them, "With men this is impossible, but with God all things are possible."
Matthew 19:26 NKJV

1. If this young man could not buy or work his way to heaven, who could? What is important about Jesus' response in verse 26?

_____

_____

_____

_____

2. Why was it so hard for the young man to do what Jesus told him?

_____

_____

_____

_____

_____

Going Deeper

In Jesus' time, people often assumed that prosperity was the result of proper obedience to God. Their wealth, in other words, was a tangible expression of their salvation. The other side of that assumption was that those who were poor must have offended God and were experiencing the consequences.

When Jesus said the young man still lacked one thing, everyone would have been surprised. How could a rich man lack some part of his salvation? Then, when Jesus invited the young man to sell his possessions so he could become one of Jesus' followers, the onlookers would have been further astounded that the man did not take him up on the offer.

With his invitation, Jesus exposed the man's true priorities.

Trivia Tidbit

According to Jewish tradition, a father will place his hands on his children and bless them on the night that begins the Sabbath, much as Jesus does for the children in this passage.

Going Deeper Questions

3. We live in an affluent place and time. In our lives, how does "stuff" get in the way of following Jesus?

_____

_____

_____

_____

4. What was Peter asking Jesus when he asked what the disciples would receive for leaving everything to follow him?

_____

_____

_____

_____

5. What does this passage say to you?

_____

_____

_____

_____

Week Five

God Wants You to Change

Day 1

Today's Scripture
Psalm 51

Key Verse

Create in me a pure heart, O God, and renew a steadfast spirit within me.

Psalm 51:10 NIV

1. What is David's prayer in verse 10 of today's Scripture? What do you understand a "steadfast spirit" to mean?

_____

_____

_____

_____

_____

2. How do you interpret verse 5 in light of what you have learned in Genesis 3 and other passages about the nature of sin? Do you believe that a bent toward sin is part of human nature or not? What evidence supports your viewpoint?

_____

_____

_____

_____

Going Deeper

This psalm is sometimes referred to as a "prayer of restoration," because it is believed that King David wrote it when he was confronted with his sins of adultery and murder. David knew that he was wrong, that he had sinned against God, and that no amount of sacrifice would cover his guilt.

David understood the sacrifice system that took place in the Tabernacle. The greater the sin, the greater the value of the animals one brought for sacrifice. David also understood something else. It was not the killing of an animal that brought forgiveness, but a true sorrow for the wrongs committed and for hurting the Lord.

David prayed for God's help to make a true change in his spirit and life. He understood that without a return to the Lord, no real change is possible.

Trivia Tidbit

At the first Passover, the Israelites used a hyssop branch dipped in lamb's blood to paint their doorways so they would be safe from God's wrath.

Going Deeper Questions

3. Have you ever tried to sacrifice something in your life to make up for past sins?

_____

_____

_____

_____

4. What does this passage teach us about the nature of forgiveness?

_____

_____

_____

_____

5. What is the "broken spirit" described in verse 17, and how can we offer it up to God as a true sacrifice?

_____

_____

_____

_____

Today's Scripture

Luke 4:1-15

Key Verse

Jesus answered, "It is written: 'Worship the Lord your God and serve him only.'"

Luke 4:8 TNIV

1. In today's Scripture, what term do verses 1 and 14 have in common? Why is this significant?

_____

_____

_____

_____

2. Why do you suppose God let Jesus experience such temptation, especially when Jesus was most vulnerable? What can we learn from Jesus' response to temptation that we can apply in our own lives?

_____

_____

_____

_____

Going Deeper

Fasting was an important part of worship for the Israelites, and it still is for Christians today. It is a chance to offer up to God something that is important to us, not as a way to gain favor or earn something from God but as a reminder that everything we have is a gift from God.

While fasting from food is often undertaken as a way of affirming our complete dependence on God, anything that is personally important can be offered to God in a fast. Sacrificing in this way, whether with food or with something else, gives us time to communicate with God in our need, understanding that God alone can supply all things.

Fasting is a discipline that can lead us into greater simplicity. If we fast from electronic devices or our usual activities, we can use that time to focus ourselves on prayer or the truths of Scripture. Depending on what we fast from, we can enjoy opportunities for silence and calm that are not present in our normal lives. As a result, God often uses these times of fasting to change us.

Trivia Tidbit

Moses, Elijah, and Jesus all fasted for forty days in a row at least once.

Interestingly, Moses and Elijah were also present at Jesus' transfiguration.

Going Deeper Questions

3. Yesterday's Scripture talked about sacrifices that were not effective. When we fast and practice other forms of spiritual sacrifice, how can we make sure these will bring us closer to God?

_____

_____

_____

_____

_____

4. What one thing in your life would be the hardest to sacrifice in a fast? How might your life be changed if you were to give that one thing up for a time? Is God calling you to do so?

_____

_____

_____

_____

_____

_____

Day 3

Today's Scripture
John 14

Key Verse

Jesus answered, "I am the way and the truth and the life. No one comes to the Father except through me."

John 14:6 NIV

1. In verses 16-17 of today's Scripture, what does Jesus tell the disciples they will be given? What distinction does Christ make about this gift?

_____

_____

_____

_____

2. In reading this passage, what do you find to be the most inviting of the promises Christ makes? Why?

_____

_____

_____

_____

_____

Going Deeper

A child stands by the side of a pool, while his father calls for him to jump in the water.

"I'll catch you," the dad promises.

The father is standing in three feet of water. He is eye level with the little boy who is standing by the side of the pool. This father has carried his son in his arms and on his shoulders all his life. But the boy won't budge. He is not jumping.

Surrender begins with trust that overcomes our fears. In today's Scripture, Jesus is talking about the greatest plunge of all—life after death. He does not begin his discussion with a grand theology of heaven or a long discussion of what awaits us there. Jesus simply says, "Don't be troubled. Trust in God. Trust also in me."

Jesus assures his listeners that he knows the way to heaven. He wants them to have confidence in their salvation. He does not want them to worry about him after his death, nor does he want them to carry anxiety about their own. He leaves them with peace and the promise that God's Spirit will be with them always.

> **Trivia Tidbit**
>
> *The Greek word translated here as "advocate" is* paraclete, *which can also mean "counselor," "intercessor," "comforter," or "helper."*

We can't experience the kinds of transformation Jesus promised in this life or the life to come until we put our trust in him. He has promised that he knows the way, that he cares for us, and that he will take us to a place he has prepared. The knowledge that Christ cares for us so deeply, and wants us to be with him eternally, can take a great deal of fear out of our thoughts of death.

Going Deeper Questions

3. When do you find it hard to trust God? What, if anything, has recently helped you learn to trust God more?

_____

_____

_____

_____

_____

4. Write a description of what you believe about heaven. What promises do you find in John 14 that bring you a sense of assurance about heaven?

_____

_____

_____

_____

_____

Today's Scripture

1 Corinthians 2

Key Verse

"For who has known the mind of the Lord so as to instruct him?" But we have the mind of Christ.

1 Corinthians 2:16 NRSV

1. In today's Scripture, what is the contrast in verses 14 and 15 between a person with the Spirit and a person without?

_____

_____

_____

_____

2. Some Bible translations subtitle this passage of Scripture "Wisdom from the Spirit." What is the difference between human wisdom and God's wisdom?

_____

_____

_____

_____

_____

Going Deeper

Corinth was a city in ancient Greece whose residents valued learning, philosophy, and wisdom. The Greeks recognized the power of the mind and were some of the finest thinkers in the world. Many of their writings are still read and shared today. But Paul wrote to the church at Corinth that if we are ever going to have the new life in Christ we desire, we will have to seek another kind of wisdom. The good news is that there is a divine wisdom to guide and direct our lives that God gives us through the Holy Spirit.

Paul wrote that the reason God's wisdom is so applicable to our lives is that God knows us as our Creator. Imagine having access to a source of wisdom that is custom-made for your particular life. Following such wisdom will be life-changing. This is what awaits those who seek the guidance of the Holy Spirit through prayer, through the reading of Scripture, and through the other disciplines of our faith.

> ### Trivia Tidbit
>
> *According to author David Malick, Paul visited Corinth at least three times and probably wrote the book of Romans over three months during his final stay in Corinth.*

Going Deeper Questions

3. What is the difference between knowledge and wisdom? What does today's Scripture say about each?

_____

_____

_____

_____

_____

_____

_____

4. What has God recently revealed about your life that will require a change of some sort? What wisdom has God revealed during prayer or reading the Scripture that is speaking to you at this time?

_____

_____

_____

_____

_____

_____

Day 5

Key Verse

Therefore, if anyone is in Christ, he is a new creation; old things have passed away; behold, all things have become new.
                                                   2 Corinthians 5:17 NKJV

1. According to verse 16 of today's Scripture, how has Paul's view, both of Christ and of people, changed?

_____

_____

_____

_____

_____

2. What is your response to the invitation to be an ambassador for Christ?

_____

_____

_____

_____

_____

Going Deeper

Paul makes an audacious claim in this chapter. He promises that through Christ, anyone can become a new creation.

Think about the implications of that statement in your life. You probably have things that you regret, memories that you try to forget but which are like bad stains on a carpet—the more you try to wash them out, the more they come back to the surface. Paul says Christ has the power to change all that: the old, he promises, is gone. You may have certain habits that you have tried and failed to change for years.

Paul tells us that Christ has the ability to bring you a new life. All of this, he says, is from God, who desires to transform us if we will accept his love and forgiveness.

Think about your life. Do you feel that over time Christ is making you into something different from the parts of your past that you regret? Are you becoming more in love with God and more loving toward your neighbor?

> **Trivia Tidbit**
>
> *Because the Roman Empire was so large, ambassadors often were sent to rebellious territories to broker peace with the citizens and quell uprisings.*

Paul was a man whose attitudes and actions had been completely changed by Christ. He wanted us to know that the same thing is available to us.

Going Deeper Questions

3. What does it mean to be reconciled to God through Christ?

_____

_____

_____

_____

_____

_____

_____

4. Where have you seen change in your life as a result of following Christ? What hinders your transformation? What will be necessary in order for you to become the new creation that Paul writes about in this passage?

_____

_____

_____

_____

_____

_____

_____

Week Six

God Wants to Be With You Forever

Day 1

Today's Scripture
Matthew 25:1-13

Key Verse
Therefore keep watch, because you do not know the day or the hour.

Matthew 25:13 NIV

1. Who does the bridegroom in today's parable represent? Who do the virgins represent? What does the oil represent? With what warning does Jesus conclude the parable?

_____

_____

_____

_____

_____

2. Consider your answer to the first question regarding the oil. Is a relationship with God something that can be borrowed? Why or why not?

_____

_____

_____

_____

_____

Going Deeper

Weddings in Jesus' day were huge community gatherings that sometimes went on for days. People ate a very plain diet, and food was not always plentiful, so the feasting that accompanied a wedding was very special. In fact, because there was little to break the monotony of daily life, a wedding was an event that few willingly would have missed.

Custom dictated, however, that you show up on time. There was no such thing as "fashionably late." Not only did the tardy guests miss the fun, but their lateness was taken as a personal insult by the host, usually the groom and his family.

> ## Trivia Tidbit
>
> *In the current Jewish wedding ceremony, the rabbi may bless a cup of wine and give it to the new couple as a symbol of their shared life to come.*

In this story, the young ladies were waiting to join the processional, where the groom would go to the bride's house and escort her back to the ceremony at his house. Since this took place in the evening, oil lamps were needed for the procession, and members of the community would join the celebration with their lamps lighting the way home.

Imagine this procession of lights around the bride and groom as they made their way to the celebration. How sad to be left out of the festivities because you didn't have enough oil to participate. Those who missed the wedding missed so much: the banquet, the fellowship, the excitement of the celebration, and the ability to talk about it later in the village.

How sad it was for them to run out of oil. . .and how much sadder for us if we allow our faith to ebb before our Groom returns!

Going Deeper Questions

3. How we look at this story depends entirely on our relationship with Christ. Does the suddenness of the groom's arrival seem distressing or exciting?

_____

_____

_____

_____

_____

_____

4. How can we be prepared for the Groom's return, when he leads the church back to his home for the marriage celebration?

_____

_____

_____

_____

_____

_____

Day 2

Key Verse

Then the master told his servant, "Go out to the roads and country lanes and compel them to come in, so that my house will be full."

Luke 14:23 NIV

1. In today's Scripture, what does verse 18 say about how the invitees responded to the banquet? List the excuses offered in verses 18-20 for not attending.

_____

_____

_____

_____

_____

2. Why do you suppose so many people, like those invited to the banquet, refuse invitations to know God?

_____

_____

_____

_____

Going Deeper

Today's Scripture is another instance of Jesus describing his kingdom as a party, and he specifically points out that the party is all-inclusive. When the original guests do not make the invitation of the host a priority, he opens his door to everyone. The host tells his servants to look everywhere for people who would enjoy his hospitality. People from every race, class, and social strata are invited.

Such an all-encompassing view of God's reign would have been a shock to Jesus' audience, who believed the invitation would only go to the Jews as God's chosen people. Jesus wanted them to understand that God's covenant with the Jews was like the first invitation, and afterward the host would not be hindered in blessing the whole world with the goodness and hospitality of heaven.

Trivia Tidbit

Feasts and festivals were a big part of the Hebrew religious calendar. In Leviticus 23 alone, God commands six annual worship events (some people count them as seven) plus a weekly Sabbath.

Going Deeper Questions

3. What excuses do we make for not spending time in God's presence? In what way are they like or different from the excuses made in the parable?

_____

_____

_____

_____

_____

_____

_____

4. We are assured that heaven is going to include all people who have a relationship with Christ. How can we be more inclusive and celebratory in the church today?

_____

_____

_____

_____

_____

_____

_____

99

Day 3

Today's Scripture

John 10:1-21

Key Verse

I am the good shepherd. The good shepherd lays down his life for the sheep.

John 10:11 HCSB

1. At the end of today's passage, the response to Jesus is much the same as we see today. What sometimes makes it hard for us to accept Jesus as Christ, Savior, and Shepherd?

_____

_____

_____

_____

2. What message of hope is found in this passage for someone who is lost? How might you share this message in your own words or through your own life experience?

_____

_____

_____

_____

Going Deeper

In Jesus' time, Israel was an agrarian society. Shepherding was one of its main occupations. Because of this, in today's Scripture Jesus was describing a world that his audience knew intimately. They understood that caring for sheep was the life of a good shepherd. The flock provided him clothing, food, and money to live on, and in exchange the shepherd gave the sheep a life they could not have found on their own. He led them to pasture and safe water and protected them with his very life if necessary.

Jesus assures us that he is our shepherd. We listen to his voice, we follow his commands, and he will lay down his life for our sake. Jesus wants us to know that he is offering us more than an existence. He wants to give us a life that is abundant now and eternally.

Trivia Tidbit

There are ten times as many sheep in New Zealand as there are people, and one man there, Simon McCorkindale, owns a record 384,143 of them!

Going Deeper Questions

3. How good are you at hearing the Good Shepherd's voice? How often do you listen for the direction of the Shepherd, and what might help you listen better?

_____

_____

_____

_____

_____

_____

_____

4. Where in your life do you feel led to help tend Christ's flock so that others will know the love and care of God?

_____

_____

_____

_____

_____

_____

_____

Day 4

Today's Scripture
John 3

Key Verse

Jesus replied, "Very truly I tell you, no one can see the kingdom of God unless they are born again."

John 3:3 NIV

1. How would you describe what Jesus is talking about in verses 3 and 5-9 of today's Scripture?

_____

_____

_____

_____

_____

2. Nicodemus was obviously an intelligent man. Why do you suppose it was so hard for him to understand what Jesus was saying?

_____

_____

_____

_____

_____

Going Deeper

It is comforting to know that a man as intelligent and well-educated in Jewish law and customs as Nicodemus still had questions about the way God works. Like many people, he believed that Jesus was a great man, a wise rabbi, and a miracle worker. He believed in the things Jesus spoke about: life in God's kingdom and even eternal life.

Nicodemus wanted to know how to have these things. He was not looking for a theoretical concept about eternal life; he wanted to know that when he died, he would go to heaven. Nicodemus believed that Jesus had this information.

Jesus answered that he was not so much a source of wisdom as a way of life. He called Nicodemus to believe in him and to be born into a new way of being. In so doing, Jesus made a bold claim, saying he could be believed because he had seen heaven. He knew what it was like and how to get there.

This is the reason that today, Christ's followers are able to live with a gentle but unflinching confidence about their life after death. We are following one who has come from heaven, who understands it fully, and who wants to take us there. That journey begins with our willingness to accept the relationship that Christ offers to us.

> **Trivia Tidbit**
>
> *The story of Moses and the snake is located in Numbers 21:4-9. When the Israelites were being bitten by poisonous snakes, God told Moses to make a bronze snake, and everyone who looked at it was saved from the poison.*

Going Deeper Questions

3. Like Nicodemus, we need to be born again. What does this passage say we must do to be saved, and how does it apply to you today?

_____

_____

_____

_____

_____

_____

_____

4. To be born again, we must come out of the darkness into the light of Jesus Christ. What things in your life do you still keep hidden in the dark? How can you bring these things into the light to find forgiveness and salvation?

_____

_____

_____

_____

_____

_____

_____

Day 5

Today's Scripture

Hebrews 12

Key Verse

Make every effort to live in peace with everyone and to be holy; without holiness no one will see the Lord.

Hebrews 12:14 TNIV

1. What important instruction is offered in verse 25 of today's Scripture? What are we directed to do in verses 28-29?

_____

_____

_____

_____

_____

2. What is easy about the instructions in verses 14-16? What is difficult?

_____

_____

_____

_____

_____

Going Deeper

Tombstones usually list a person's date of birth and date of death. Everything in between is represented by a dash. One speaker suggested that it is important to ask what we are putting in the dash between those two dates. That is true for our life in Christ as well. There is quite a distance between the moment we accept Christ and the moment we die and enter the gates of heaven.

> ## Trivia Tidbit
> *Hebrews 12:18-21 is referring to Mount Sinai. This is one of the most frequently mentioned mountains in the Bible and is sometimes called Mount Horeb or Mount Musa (which can be translated as "Mount Moses").*

Preparing to enter heaven requires a kind of humility seen in today's Scripture as it describes how the people of Israel reacted when they perceived God's presence on the mountain. They realized that God was holy and divine and they were sinful and human, but that realization did not end their relationship with God. In fact, it enabled a real relationship of trust and dependence to begin.

Moving toward heaven requires the persistence of a distance runner in a cross-country race. The terrain is varied. It includes steep hills, flowing streams, and the occasional gentle slope.

No matter what comes at us in life, the author of Hebrews calls us persistently to pursue our love of God. That pursuit requires a willingness to keep Christ before us, to fix our gaze on the goal so we will continue to strive for the things of God.

Most people will state a desire to go to heaven. The author of Hebrews calls us to consider the journey to the finish line.

Going Deeper Questions

3. One definition of holiness is to be dedicated to God. How can God use our struggles with sin to build perseverance and make us holy?

_____

_____

_____

_____

_____

_____

_____

4. Where in your life do you need to be more disciplined in your faith, your actions, and your thoughts? Once you identify the problem areas, how can you better address and overcome them?

_____

_____

_____

_____

_____

_____

Notes

The following notes offer citations for the Trivia Tidbits found throughout this book. They are listed by week and day—for example, "4.1" means the Tidbit for week 4, day 1.

1.1—From the BBC Science website, accessed February 4, 2014 (http://www.bbc.co.uk/science/humanbody/body/factfiles/bonegrowth/femur.shtml).

1.2—The uses can be counted in any good concordance. The exact number may vary depending on the translation.

1.3—"Makarios," in *The NAS New Testament Greek Lexicon*, accessed February 12, 2014 (http://www.biblestudytools.com/lexicons/greek/nas/makarios.html) and in Liddel and Scott's *Greek-English Lexicon*, accessed February 12, 2014 (http://stephanus.tlg.uci.edu/lsj/).

1.4—A search for "drachma denarius" at http://www.perseus.tufts.edu/hopper/ (accessed February 12, 2014) will provide several sources comparing the two coins.

1.5—Stephen L. Harris, "The Gospels," in *Understanding the Bible*, 2nd ed. (Palo Alto: Mayfield, 1985), pp. 266-68.

2.1—James Henry Breasted, *Ancient Times, a History of the Early World: An Introduction to the Study of Ancient History and the Career of Early Man* (Boston: Ginn, 1916), pp. 108-11.

2.2—"Wine and Rome," in the *Encyclopedia Romana*, accessed February 4, 2014 (http://penelope.uchicago.edu/~grout/encyclopaedia_romana/wine/wine.html).

2.3—Joel Kalvesmaki, "Table of Old Testament Quotes in the New Testament, in English Translation," Septuagint Online, accessed February 4, 2014 (http://www.kalvesmaki.com/LXX/NTChart.htm).

2.4—George Arthur Buttrick, ed., "Water," in *The Interpreter's Dictionary of the Bible*, vol. 4 (New York: Abingdon Press, 1962), p. 806.

2.5—M. G. Easton, "Praetorium," in *Illustrated Bible Dictionary*, 3rd ed. (London, Edinburgh, and New York: Thomas Nelson, 1897).

3.1—David N. Bivin, "The Miraculous Catch: Reflections on the Research of Mendel Nun" (1992), accessed February 12, 2014 (http://www.jerusalemperspective.com/2644/).

3.2—*God's Game Plan: The Athletes' Bible*, Holman Christian Standard Version (Nashville: Holman Bible Publishers, 2005), p. NT208.

3.3—See Leviticus 16.

3.4—*God's Game Plan: The Athlete's Bible*, p. NT89.

3.5—"Chara" and "Charis" in *The KJV New Testament Greek Lexicon*, accessed February 13, 2014 (http://www.biblestudytools.com/lexicons/greek/kjv/chara.html and http://www.biblestudytools.com/lexicons/greek/kjv/charis.html).

4.1—See Genesis 3:24; Ezekiel 1:4-14; 10:20-22; 41:18-19.

4.2—"Diaspora," in Liddel and Scott's *Greek-English Lexicon*, accessed February 13, 2014 (http://stephanus.tlg.uci.edu/lsj/); Mattis Kantor, *The Jewish Time Line Encyclopedia: A Year-by-Year History from Creation to the Present,* updated ed., (Northvale, NJ: Jason Aronson, 1992).

4.3—Compare Matthew, Mark, and Luke with John.

4.4—David Padfield, "The Biblical Cities of Laodicia, Colosse, and Hierapolis" (2005), accessed February 4, 2014 (http://www.padfield.com/acrobat/history/laodicea.pdf).

4.5—"Shabbat: Shabbat Evening Home Rituals," accessed February 4, 2014 (http://www.jewishvirtuallibrary.org/jsource/Judaism/Shabbat2.html#4).

5.1—See Exodus 12.

5.2—See Exodus 34:28; 1 Kings 19:7-9; Matthew 17:1-8.

5.3—"Who or What Is the Advocate or Counselor?" accessed February 4, 2014 (http://bibleq.net/answer/759/).

5.4—David Malick, "An Introduction to the Book of Romans," accessed February 13, 2014 (https://bible.org/article/introduction-book-romans).

5.5—*God's Game Plan: The Athletes' Bible,* p. 250.

6.1—"Jewish Wedding," accessed February 4, 2014 (http://www. jewishweddingtraditions.org/).

6.2—See Leviticus 23.

6.3—"Story: Sheep Farming," in *Te Ara Encyclopedia of New Zealand*, accessed February 13, 2014 (http://www.teara.govt.nz/en/sheep-farming); "Sheep Farming," accessed February 4, 2014 (http://en.wikipedia.org/ wiki/Sheep_farming).

6.4—See Numbers 21:4-9.

6.5—J. Rendel Harris, "Sinai, Mount," in James Hastings, *A Dictionary of the Bible* (New York: Scribner's, 1901–1902), 4:537 (http://www.ccel.org/ccel/ hastings/dictv4/Page_537.html); "Mount Horeb," in *Jewish Encyclopedia* (New York: Funk and Wagnalls, 1901–1906), accessed February 4, 2014 (http://www.jewishencyclopedia.com/articles/13766-sinai-mount).